mom & me

AN INTERACTIVE JOURNAL
TO LEARN MORE ABOUT EACH OTHER

chartwell
books

DATE STARTED:

NAME:

WHAT YOU CALL ME:

NAME:

WHAT YOU CALL ME:

INTRODUCTION

Mothers and their children share a very special bond. Get to know each other better and learn all the wonderful details about a person you already love. This journal is a space for the both to grow a deeper sense of connection while having some fun along the way. This side-by-side art journal is intended to help you and your child open the lines of communication for more meaningful conversations and learn more about each other through the mediums of art and writing.

Journaling together is something that you might want to do regularly. Think about setting aside some time every week (or even every day!) to create together and talk about whatever comes up.

There are many different types of journal entries here, some that require complete sentences, others where you circle your answers, and then a few two-page spreads where the two of you can draw and let your creativity flow. With 200 pages filled with different journaling activities, the topics in the prompts range from identifying and expressing feelings and exploring hopes and dreams to whether or not you like pickles and sour candy. Read the prompt together, and once you understand it, write down, circle, or draw your responses and then compare the two.

HOW TO USE THIS JOURNAL

You may have noticed that there are no chapters in this book. Only a vast spread of pages with varying themes and styles. Go through the journal from front to back or skip through and pick the most compelling pages for you and your child.

Journaling with your child is something that you may want to do together regularly. Think about setting aside time every day or every week to create art together and discuss what it brings up for you. Or use this book when a prompt's topic may relate to something that your child or your family is encountering at that moment. The theme of the prompt may bring about a discussion while you both are working, which is terrific; however, it's also okay to work in silence and then talk about what you created when you're finished.

Remember, regardless of artistic experience, there is no right or wrong way to respond to a prompt. The key to successful communication with each other is to be open and use the prompt to start a larger conversation. The quality of the art or the writing is immaterial; it is the quality of the conversation that you will both cherish.

If your child isn't ready for a conversation, don't put pressure on him or her. When your child is ready and comfortable, he or she may begin sharing. Every child has a different pace or comfort level. Most of all, enjoy your time together as you learn more about each other art journaling side by side, and once you finish all the prompts, you'll forever have a wonderful shared journal that you created together!

★ FOR MOM ★

This journal offers you the opportunity to learn about the person your child is becoming and to share who you are, outside of being a mom. There is space for you to look back at your own hopes as you first stepped out into the world and to dream about your future, as well as to connect through memories and understand how your child sees the world and what they want from life.

Here is a place for your child to communicate with you about the little things and the big things in their world. Use these pages to learn more about your child and to share with your child your own deepest beliefs—but reserve judgment and don't use this space to lecture. Instead, view the journal entries as jumping-off points for deeper conversations, either to problem-solve or so you can act as a sounding board.

Though your baby will always be your baby, your child is always growing and this is an excellent way to make sure you know who they are every step of the way. Dive in and learn more about this fabulous person you've helped create!

★ FOR ME ★

Your mom will always be your mom—your biggest cheerleader and most loyal supporter—but she can also become a treasured friend and confidant. Jump in and find out more about the amazing woman she is.

Learn all about her and use this space to share what is going on in your head.

YOU AND ME

SPECIAL MEMORIES
WE'VE MADE TOGETHER

MOM: ME:

THREE FABULOUS THINGS ABOUT BEING YOUR MOM:

1

~~~~~~

2

~~~~~~

3

THREE FABULOUS THINGS ABOUT HAVING YOU AS MY MOM:

1

~~~~~~

2

~~~~~~

3

~~~~~~

MOM

FOR EACH ENTRY, WRITE A TYPE YOU LIKE
AND A TYPE YOU DISLIKE.

	LIKE	AND	DISLIKE
BREAKFAST			
DONUT			
LUNCH			
FAST FOOD			
SNACK			
DINNER			
CUISINE			
DESSERT			
ICE CREAM FLAVOR			
COOKIE			
CANDY			

ME

FOR EACH ENTRY, WRITE A TYPE YOU LIKE AND A TYPE YOU DISLIKE.

LIKE AND DISLIKE

BREAKFAST

DONUT

LUNCH

FAST FOOD

SNACK

DINNER

CUISINE

DESSERT

ICE CREAM FLAVOR

COOKIE

CANDY

DESCRIBE YOUR EARLIEST MEMORY. WHAT WERE YOU DOING?

WHO ELSE WAS THERE?

DESCRIBE YOUR EARLIEST MEMORY. WHAT WERE YOU DOING?

WHO ELSE WAS THERE?

IF OUR FAMILY HAD A...

· MOM ·   · ME ·

THEME
SONG

MASCOT

SIGNATURE
COLOR

SPORT

NICKNAME

SHARE A PROUD FAMILY MOMENT.

MOM:

ME:

CIRCLE YOUR ANSWERS

THEN POSE YOUR OWN QUESTIONS ON THE
OPPOSITE PAGE FOR YOUR JOURNAL MATE.

WOULD YOU RATHER...

Become a two-inch-tall fairy or
a 20-foot-tall giant?

Art or sports?

Mall or park?

Eat at a restaurant or order takeout?

Cut your hair at home or
do your nails at home?

Vampires or werewolves?

Live in your favorite book universe or
movie universe?

Libraries or stadiums?

1

2

3

4

5

6

· MOM ·

1

2

3

4

5

6

CIRCLE YOUR ANSWERS

THEN POSE YOUR OWN QUESTIONS ON THE
OPPOSITE PAGE FOR YOUR JOURNAL MATE.

WOULD YOU RATHER...

Become a two-inch-tall fairy or
a 20-foot-tall giant?

Art or sports?

mall or park?

Eat at a restaurant or order takeout?

cut your hair at home or
do your nails at home?

vampires or werewolves?

Live in your favorite book universe or
movie universe?

Libraries or stadiums?

Draw a treasure map full of obstacles, landmarks, and characters that you must pass to find the treasure.

· MOM ·

· ME ·

SONGS ON MY ROAD TRIP PLAYLIST:

THE BEST DAY TRIP:

THE BEST SOUVENIR I'VE EVER BOUGHT:

SONGS ON MY ROAD TRIP PLAYLIST:

THE BEST DAY TRIP:

THE BEST SOUVENIR I'VE EVER BOUGHT:

YOU ARE GIVEN A QUEST, WHICH WILL BE DANGEROUS WITH MANY DIFFICULT PROBLEMS TO SOLVE. WHO WILL YOU PUT ON A TEAM OF FIVE PEOPLE TO HELP YOU?

1

2

3

4

5

YOU ARE GIVEN A QUEST, WHICH WILL BE DANGEROUS WITH MANY DIFFICULT PROBLEMS TO SOLVE. WHO WILL YOU PUT ON A TEAM OF FIVE PEOPLE TO HELP YOU?

1

~~~~~~

2

~~~~~~

3

~~~~~~

4

~~~~~~

5

~~~~~~

1 ----- TO ----- 10

1	2	3	4	5	6	7	8	9	10	POP MUSIC
1	2	3	4	5	6	7	8	9	10	CLASSICAL MUSIC
1	2	3	4	5	6	7	8	9	10	FRUIT CAKE
1	2	3	4	5	6	7	8	9	10	THUNDER& LIGHTNING
1	2	3	4	5	6	7	8	9	10	REPTILES
1	2	3	4	5	6	7	8	9	10	MATH
1	2	3	4	5	6	7	8	9	10	STARGAZING
1	2	3	4	5	6	7	8	9	10	SUNRISE
1	2	3	4	5	6	7	8	9	10	COMIC BOOKS
1	2	3	4	5	6	7	8	9	10	SUGAR COOKIES
1	2	3	4	5	6	7	8	9	10	BASKETBALL
1	2	3	4	5	6	7	8	9	10	BROCCOLI
1	2	3	4	5	6	7	8	9	10	TIGERS
1	2	3	4	5	6	7	8	9	10	CAMPING
1	2	3	4	5	6	7	8	9	10	FUZZY SOCKS
1	2	3	4	5	6	7	8	9	10	ORANGE JUICE

RATE THE FOLLOWING THINGS, FROM ONE TO TEN, AND COMPARE YOUR ANSWERS.

1 2 3 4 5 6 7 8 9 10	POP MUSIC
1 2 3 4 5 6 7 8 9 10	CLASSICAL MUSIC
1 2 3 4 5 6 7 8 9 10	FRUIT CAKE
1 2 3 4 5 6 7 8 9 10	THUNDER & LIGHTNING
1 2 3 4 5 6 7 8 9 10	REPTILES
1 2 3 4 5 6 7 8 9 10	MATH
1 2 3 4 5 6 7 8 9 10	STARGAZING
1 2 3 4 5 6 7 8 9 10	SUNRISE
1 2 3 4 5 6 7 8 9 10	COMIC BOOKS
1 2 3 4 5 6 7 8 9 10	SUGAR COOKIES
1 2 3 4 5 6 7 8 9 10	BASKETBALL
1 2 3 4 5 6 7 8 9 10	BROCCOLI
1 2 3 4 5 6 7 8 9 10	TIGERS
1 2 3 4 5 6 7 8 9 10	CAMPING
1 2 3 4 5 6 7 8 9 10	FUZZY SOCKS
1 2 3 4 5 6 7 8 9 10	ORANGE JUICE

WHAT SPORT WOULD YOU LIKE TO GO TO THE OLYMPICS
FOR, AND WHAT DO YOU IMAGINE IT WOULD BE LIKE?

....

....

....

....

....

....

DRAW YOURSELF AS AN ELITE ATHLETE.

WHAT SPORT WOULD YOU LIKE TO GO TO THE OLYMPICS
FOR, AND WHAT DO YOU IMAGINE IT WOULD BE LIKE?

....
....
....
....
....
....

DRAW YOURSELF AS AN ELITE ATHLETE.

· ADVENTURE LIST ·

· MOM ·   · ME ·

	SWING DANCING	
	○ MOM ○ ME	
	YOGA	
	○ MOM ○ ME	
	BAKING	
	○ MOM ○ ME	
	BUG HUNTING	
	○ MOM ○ ME	
	POTTERY	
	○ MOM ○ ME	
	SKY DIVING	
	○ MOM ○ ME	
	HULA HOOP	
	○ MOM ○ ME	
	SOCCER	
	○ MOM ○ ME	
	BASKETBALL	
	○ MOM ○ ME	

WRITE "YES" OR "NO" IN YOUR COLUMN FOR THESE
ACTIVITIES AND ADVENTURES YOU'D LIKE TO TRY
SOMEDAY. IF YOU BOTH WANT TO DO SOMETHING, DO IT
TOGETHER! IF YOU'VE ALREADY DONE IT, CHECK IT OFF.

· MOM ·   · ME ·

	ENGLISH TEA PARTY	
	◯ MOM ◯ ME	
	CLAY CRAFTS	
	◯ MOM ◯ ME	
	FACE PAINTING	
	◯ MOM ◯ ME	
	SEWING	
	◯ MOM ◯ ME	
	BASEBALL GAME	
	◯ MOM ◯ ME	
	PAPER MACHE FACE	
	◯ MOM ◯ ME	
	CANDLE MAKING	
	◯ MOM ◯ ME	
	A BIG PUZZLE	
	◯ MOM ◯ ME	
	TREE CLIMBING	
	◯ MOM ◯ ME	

WHAT WOULD YOU SAY OUR FAMILY'S MOTTO IS?

HOW DO WE SHOW THIS?

WHAT WOULD YOU SAY OUR FAMILY'S MOTTO IS?

HOW DO WE SHOW THIS?

A coat of arms is a centuries-old design created to represent families. Design your family's crest.

· MOM ·

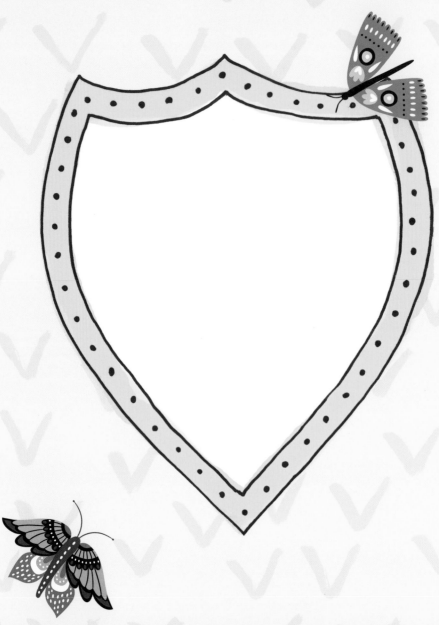

consider the traits, interests, and talents
that make your family unique and add them
to the shield.

· ME ·

1 ---TO--- 10

1	2	3	4	5	6	7	8	9	10	SWEET CEREAL
1	2	3	4	5	6	7	8	9	10	SCARY MOVIES
1	2	3	4	5	6	7	8	9	10	DINOSAURS
1	2	3	4	5	6	7	8	9	10	FRIED CHICKEN
1	2	3	4	5	6	7	8	9	10	SWIMMING
1	2	3	4	5	6	7	8	9	10	PUMPKIN PIE
1	2	3	4	5	6	7	8	9	10	WATERFALLS
1	2	3	4	5	6	7	8	9	10	CARD GAMES
1	2	3	4	5	6	7	8	9	10	GRAPE JUICE
1	2	3	4	5	6	7	8	9	10	STUFFED ANIMALS
1	2	3	4	5	6	7	8	9	10	SEQUINS
1	2	3	4	5	6	7	8	9	10	FANCY SNEAKERS
1	2	3	4	5	6	7	8	9	10	THE SMELL OF RAIN
1	2	3	4	5	6	7	8	9	10	FLIP FLOPS
1	2	3	4	5	6	7	8	9	10	HORSEBACK RIDING
1	2	3	4	5	6	7	8	9	10	FISHING

RATE THE FOLLOWING THINGS,
FROM ONE TO TEN,
AND COMPARE YOUR ANSWERS.

1 2 3 4 5 6 7 8 9 10										SWEET CEREAL
1 2 3 4 5 6 7 8 9 10										SCARY MOVIES
1 2 3 4 5 6 7 8 9 10										DINOSAURS
1 2 3 4 5 6 7 8 9 10										FRIED CHICKEN
1 2 3 4 5 6 7 8 9 10										SWIMMING
1 2 3 4 5 6 7 8 9 10										PUMPKIN PIE
1 2 3 4 5 6 7 8 9 10										WATERFALLS
1 2 3 4 5 6 7 8 9 10										CARD GAMES
1 2 3 4 5 6 7 8 9 10										GRAPE JUICE
1 2 3 4 5 6 7 8 9 10										STUFFED ANIMALS
1 2 3 4 5 6 7 8 9 10										SEQUINS
1 2 3 4 5 6 7 8 9 10										FANCY SNEAKERS
1 2 3 4 5 6 7 8 9 10										THE SMELL OF RAIN
1 2 3 4 5 6 7 8 9 10										FLIP FLOPS
1 2 3 4 5 6 7 8 9 10										HORSEBACK RIDING
1 2 3 4 5 6 7 8 9 10										FISHING

many of us do things that we think are worthy of recognition. we can be proud of the many positive things we accomplish.

· MOM ·

YOU ARE
AWESOME!

HOORAY!

Draw the most meaningful thing you have done that you feel is award worthy.

· ME ·

HOORAY!

YOU ARE AWESOME!

CIRCLE YOUR ANSWERS

THEN POSE YOUR OWN QUESTIONS ON THE OPPOSITE PAGE FOR YOUR JOURNAL MATE.

WOULD YOU RATHER...

Breakfast or Brunch?

sweet candy or sour candy?

Horses or Fish?

Pasta or Pizza?

Red or Blue?

Eat dessert for every meal
or never eat dessert?

cloud gazing or star gazing?

sunny days or rainy days?

1

2

3

4

5

6

· MOM ·

1

2

3

4

5

6

42

CIRCLE YOUR ANSWERS

THEN POSE YOUR OWN QUESTIONS ON THE
OPPOSITE PAGE FOR YOUR JOURNAL MATE.

WOULD YOU RATHER...

Breakfast or Brunch?

sweet candy or sour candy?

Horses or Fish?

Pasta or Pizza?

Red or Blue?

Eat dessert for every meal
or never eat dessert?

cloud gazing or star gazing?

sunny days or rainy days?

NAME A FAMILY MEMBER WHO

· MOM ·

MOTIVATES YOU:

HAS THE MOST
UNIQUE LAUGH:

ALWAYS HOSTS
THE GET-
TOGETHERS:

HAS THE
BEST HOLIDAY
DECORATIONS:

KNOWS THE
MOST PEOPLE:

HAS THE
MOST PETS:

NAME A FAMILY MEMBER WHO

· ME ·

MOTIVATES YOU:

HAS THE MOST
UNIQUE LAUGH:

ALWAYS HOSTS
THE GET-
TOGETHERS:

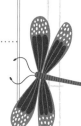

HAS THE
BEST HOLIDAY
DECORATIONS:

KNOWS THE
MOST PEOPLE:

HAS THE
MOST PETS:

✓ LIKE OR X DISLIKE?

✓ OR X WHETHER YOU LIKE OR DISLIKE
SOMETHING IN YOUR COLUMN FOR EACH ENTRY.

	· MOM ·	· ME ·
ARCADES		
LONG WEEKENDS		
POTTED PLANTS		
PINEAPPLE ON PIZZA		
SUMMER OLYMPICS		
TRAVEL		
STUFFED PLUSHIES		
MUSICALS		
PHOTOGRAPHY		
SUSHI		

46

THINGS WE ENJOY AS A FAMILY

	· MOM ·	· ME ·
MOVIES	1	1
	2	2
	3	3
GAMES	1	1
	2	2
	3	3
FESTIVALS & FAIRS	1	1
	2	2
	3	3

Use the blank comic
strip to create
a story using
original characters.

what is your
story trying
to say?

THE MOST DISGUSTING THING IN OUR HOUSE:

BEST THING IN OUR HOUSE:

FAVORITE NEIGHBOR:

THE MOST DISGUSTING THING IN OUR HOUSE:

BEST THING IN OUR HOUSE:

FAVORITE NEIGHBOR:

WHAT MYTHICAL OR MAGICAL CREATURE WOULD
YOU LIKE TO KEEP AS A PET?

WHAT WOULD YOU NAME IT?

WHAT MYTHICAL OR MAGICAL CREATURE WOULD
YOU LIKE TO KEEP AS A PET?

....

....

....

....

....

....

....

....

WHAT WOULD YOU NAME IT?

....

....

....

....

....

....

....

....

Fears can be both big or small; their size doesn't matter, because they are very real, regardless of their size.

· MOM ·

 COURAGE

Draw yourself overcoming your biggest fears.

· ME ·

COURAGE

WHEN I WAS YOUR AGE...

I LIVED IN:

I LIVED WITH:

I WENT TO
SCHOOL AT:

MY BEST
FRIENDS
WERE:

I WANTED
TO HAVE
THIS MANY
CHILDREN:

I PLANNED
TO WORK AS:

I THOUGHT I
WOULD BE:

WHEN I AM YOUR AGE...

I HOPE TO
LIVE IN:

I EXPECT TO
LIVE WITH:

I WILL
PROBABLY
HAVE
GRADUATED
FROM:

I'LL STILL
BE FRIENDS
WITH:

I WANT
TO HAVE
THIS MANY
CHILDREN:

I PLAN TO
HAVE A JOB
AS:

I THINK I
WILL BE:

57

· MOM ·

1 -----TO----- 10

1 2 3 4 5 6 7 8 9 10	SPORTS CARS
1 2 3 4 5 6 7 8 9 10	DOUBLE RAINBOWS
1 2 3 4 5 6 7 8 9 10	MICE
1 2 3 4 5 6 7 8 9 10	BIG CITIES
1 2 3 4 5 6 7 8 9 10	MALLS
1 2 3 4 5 6 7 8 9 10	PALM TREES
1 2 3 4 5 6 7 8 9 10	FRUITY CANDY
1 2 3 4 5 6 7 8 9 10	FRENCH FRIES
1 2 3 4 5 6 7 8 9 10	TOY STORES
1 2 3 4 5 6 7 8 9 10	LEMONADE
1 2 3 4 5 6 7 8 9 10	SKATEBOARDING
1 2 3 4 5 6 7 8 9 10	SEA FOOD
1 2 3 4 5 6 7 8 9 10	SCRAPBOOKING
1 2 3 4 5 6 7 8 9 10	FROZEN YOGURT
1 2 3 4 5 6 7 8 9 10	SCENTED CANDLES
1 2 3 4 5 6 7 8 9 10	ROLLER COASTERS

RATE THE FOLLOWING THINGS,
FROM ONE TO TEN,
AND COMPARE YOUR ANSWERS.

1	2	3	4	5	6	7	8	9	10	SPORTS CARS
1	2	3	4	5	6	7	8	9	10	DOUBLE RAINBOWS
1	2	3	4	5	6	7	8	9	10	MICE
1	2	3	4	5	6	7	8	9	10	BIG CITIES
1	2	3	4	5	6	7	8	9	10	MALLS
1	2	3	4	5	6	7	8	9	10	PALM TREES
1	2	3	4	5	6	7	8	9	10	FRUITY CANDY
1	2	3	4	5	6	7	8	9	10	FRENCH FRIES
1	2	3	4	5	6	7	8	9	10	TOY STORES
1	2	3	4	5	6	7	8	9	10	LEMONADE
1	2	3	4	5	6	7	8	9	10	SKATEBOARDING
1	2	3	4	5	6	7	8	9	10	SEA FOOD
1	2	3	4	5	6	7	8	9	10	SCRAPBOOKING
1	2	3	4	5	6	7	8	9	10	FROZEN YOGURT
1	2	3	4	5	6	7	8	9	10	SCENTED CANDLES
1	2	3	4	5	6	7	8	9	10	ROLLER COASTERS

ADVENTURE LIST

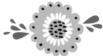

· MOM ·   · ME ·

	TRAIN TOUR	
	○ MOM ○ ME	
	HISTORIC VILLAGE	
	○ MOM ○ ME	
	SCIENCE FAIR	
	○ MOM ○ ME	
	RENAISSANCE FAIR	
	○ MOM ○ ME	
	ART GALLERY	
	○ MOM ○ ME	
	THE ZOO	
	○ MOM ○ ME	
	AQUARIUM	
	○ MOM ○ ME	
	MUSEUM	
	○ MOM ○ ME	
	OBSERVATORY	
	○ MOM ○ ME	

WRITE "YES" OR "NO" IN YOUR COLUMN FOR THESE
ACTIVITIES AND ADVENTURES YOU'D LIKE TO TRY
SOMEDAY. IF YOU BOTH WANT TO DO SOMETHING, DO IT
TOGETHER! IF YOU'VE ALREADY DONE IT, CHECK IT OFF.

· MOM ·   · ME ·

	NATIONAL PARK	
	◯ MOM ◯ ME	
	SAILING	
	◯ MOM ◯ ME	
	SKY DIVING	
	◯ MOM ◯ ME	
	OCEAN DIVING	
	◯ MOM ◯ ME	
	SNORKELING	
	◯ MOM ◯ ME	
	SAFARI	
	◯ MOM ◯ ME	
	ROCK CLIMBING	
	◯ MOM ◯ ME	
	GONDOLA RIDE	
	◯ MOM ◯ ME	
	NASCAR RACE	
	◯ MOM ◯ ME	

draw what you are thankful to have in your life.

i am THANKFUL ·FOR·

Draw what you are thankful to have in your life.

i am THANKFUL FOR

WHAT IS THE BEST PART OF BEING THE AGE YOU ARE NOW?

WHAT ARE YOU LOOKING FORWARD TO IN THE FUTURE?

WHAT IS THE BEST PART OF BEING THE AGE YOU ARE NOW?

WHAT ARE YOU LOOKING FORWARD TO IN THE FUTURE?

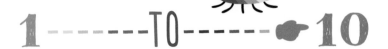

1 ----TO---- 10

1	2	3	4	5	6	7	8	9	10	GELATO
1	2	3	4	5	6	7	8	9	10	SPIDERS
1	2	3	4	5	6	7	8	9	10	AIRPLANES
1	2	3	4	5	6	7	8	9	10	SNOWSTORMS
1	2	3	4	5	6	7	8	9	10	BOOKSTORES
1	2	3	4	5	6	7	8	9	10	BEACHES
1	2	3	4	5	6	7	8	9	10	SUNBATHING
1	2	3	4	5	6	7	8	9	10	CHOCOLATE MILK
1	2	3	4	5	6	7	8	9	10	BOY BANDS
1	2	3	4	5	6	7	8	9	10	GARDENING
1	2	3	4	5	6	7	8	9	10	HIKING
1	2	3	4	5	6	7	8	9	10	DARK CHOCOLATE
1	2	3	4	5	6	7	8	9	10	BATS
1	2	3	4	5	6	7	8	9	10	ROLLER SKATING
1	2	3	4	5	6	7	8	9	10	VIDEO GAMES
1	2	3	4	5	6	7	8	9	10	PICKLES

RATE THE FOLLOWING THINGS, FROM ONE TO TEN, AND COMPARE YOUR ANSWERS.

1	2	3	4	5	6	7	8	9	10	GELATO
1	2	3	4	5	6	7	8	9	10	SPIDERS
1	2	3	4	5	6	7	8	9	10	AIRPLANES
1	2	3	4	5	6	7	8	9	10	SNOWSTORMS
1	2	3	4	5	6	7	8	9	10	BOOKSTORES
1	2	3	4	5	6	7	8	9	10	BEACHES
1	2	3	4	5	6	7	8	9	10	SUNBATHING
1	2	3	4	5	6	7	8	9	10	CHOCOLATE MILK
1	2	3	4	5	6	7	8	9	10	BOY BANDS
1	2	3	4	5	6	7	8	9	10	GARDENING
1	2	3	4	5	6	7	8	9	10	HIKING
1	2	3	4	5	6	7	8	9	10	DARK CHOCOLATE
1	2	3	4	5	6	7	8	9	10	BATS
1	2	3	4	5	6	7	8	9	10	ROLLER SKATING
1	2	3	4	5	6	7	8	9	10	VIDEO GAMES
1	2	3	4	5	6	7	8	9	10	PICKLES

FUN THINGS I LIKE TO CALL YOU

· MOM ·

1

2

3

· ME ·

1

2

3

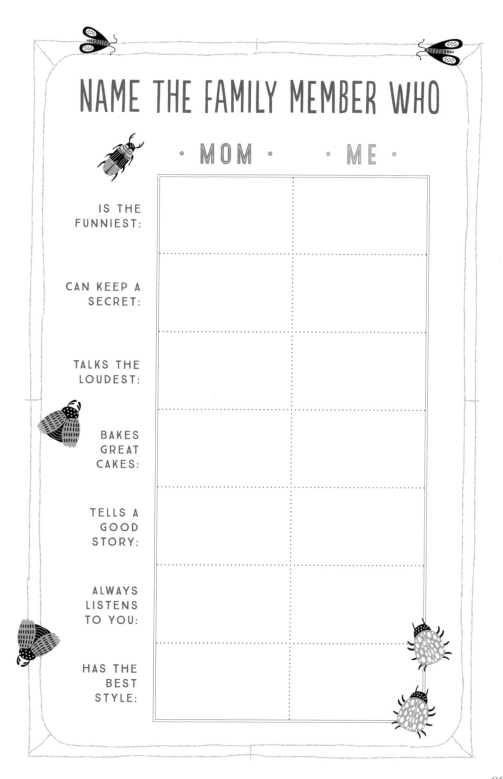

NAME THE FAMILY MEMBER WHO

· MOM ·   · ME ·

IS THE
FUNNIEST:

CAN KEEP A
SECRET:

TALKS THE
LOUDEST:

BAKES
GREAT
CAKES:

TELLS A
GOOD
STORY:

ALWAYS
LISTENS
TO YOU:

HAS THE
BEST
STYLE:

DESCRIBE SOMETHING YOU'RE LOOKING FORWARD TO.

WHAT ABOUT IT MAKES YOU MOST EXCITED?

DESCRIBE SOMETHING YOU'RE LOOKING FORWARD TO.

WHAT ABOUT IT MAKES YOU MOST EXCITED?

Imagine you owned a private island. What kind of things would you want to have on your island?

MOM

who would be there? How would you get to
the island?

Draw what your dream island would look like.

· ME ·

WHAT DO YOU REMEMBER FROM YOUR FIRST DAY OF SCHOOL?

HOW DO YOU THINK IT WILL DIFFER FROM YOUR CHILD'S?

WHAT DO YOU REMEMBER FROM YOUR FIRST DAY OF SCHOOL?

HOW DO YOU THINK IT DIFFERS FROM YOUR MOM'S?

· MOM ·

Think about a day in your life when you experienced something you will never forget. Draw that memory.

· ME ·

CIRCLE YOUR ANSWERS
THEN POSE YOUR OWN QUESTIONS ON THE
OPPOSITE PAGE FOR YOUR JOURNAL MATE.

WOULD YOU RATHER...

Apple pie or pumpkin pie?

cat or dog?

stripes or polka dots?

Hotdog or hamburger?

silver or gold?

Batman or superman?

mcDonald's or Burger King?

Be a pet cat or a wild tiger?

1

2

3

4

5

6

1

2

3

4

5

6

CIRCLE YOUR ANSWERS

THEN POSE YOUR OWN QUESTIONS ON THE
OPPOSITE PAGE FOR YOUR JOURNAL MATE.

WOULD YOU RATHER...

Apple pie or pumpkin pie?

cat or dog?

stripes or polka dots?

Hotdog or hamburger?

Silver or gold?

Batman or superman?

mcDonald's or Burger King?

Be a pet cat or a wild tiger?

1 ----TO---- 10

1	2	3	4	5	6	7	8	9	10		PUZZLES
1	2	3	4	5	6	7	8	9	10		NACHOS
1	2	3	4	5	6	7	8	9	10		DRAWING
1	2	3	4	5	6	7	8	9	10		GROWING YOUR OWN FOOD
1	2	3	4	5	6	7	8	9	10		SUMMERTIME
1	2	3	4	5	6	7	8	9	10		COLORFUL PENS
1	2	3	4	5	6	7	8	9	10		SCIENCE
1	2	3	4	5	6	7	8	9	10		RABBITS
1	2	3	4	5	6	7	8	9	10		WARM BREAD
1	2	3	4	5	6	7	8	9	10		WRITING IN A JOURNAL
1	2	3	4	5	6	7	8	9	10		TRYING NEW FOODS
1	2	3	4	5	6	7	8	9	10		SMOOTHIES
1	2	3	4	5	6	7	8	9	10		ZOMBIES
1	2	3	4	5	6	7	8	9	10		FOOTBALL
1	2	3	4	5	6	7	8	9	10		SALSA
1	2	3	4	5	6	7	8	9	10		TRAINS

RATE THE FOLLOWING THINGS,
FROM ONE TO TEN,
AND COMPARE YOUR ANSWERS.

1 2 3 4 5 6 7 8 9 10	PUZZLES
1 2 3 4 5 6 7 8 9 10	NACHOS
1 2 3 4 5 6 7 8 9 10	DRAWING
1 2 3 4 5 6 7 8 9 10	GROWING YOUR OWN FOOD
1 2 3 4 5 6 7 8 9 10	SUMMERTIME
1 2 3 4 5 6 7 8 9 10	COLORFUL PENS
1 2 3 4 5 6 7 8 9 10	SCIENCE
1 2 3 4 5 6 7 8 9 10	RABBITS
1 2 3 4 5 6 7 8 9 10	WARM BREAD
1 2 3 4 5 6 7 8 9 10	WRITING IN A JOURNAL
1 2 3 4 5 6 7 8 9 10	TRYING NEW FOODS
1 2 3 4 5 6 7 8 9 10	SMOOTHIES
1 2 3 4 5 6 7 8 9 10	ZOMBIES
1 2 3 4 5 6 7 8 9 10	FOOTBALL
1 2 3 4 5 6 7 8 9 10	SALSA
1 2 3 4 5 6 7 8 9 10	TRAINS

IF YOU COULD CHOOSE FIVE THINGS TO NEVER DO AGAIN, WHAT WOULD THEY BE?

· MOM ·

1

2

3

4

5

HELLO?

· ME ·

1

2

3

4

5

1

~~~~~~

2

~~~~~~

3

· ME ·   FAVORITE QUOTES

1

~~~~~~

2

~~~~~~

3

~~~~~~

This is a magic door that can take you anywhere.

· MOM ·

Draw what you see on the other side.

· ME ·

WHAT WOULD YOUR DAY BE LIKE IF THERE WERE NO ELECTRICITY IN THE WORLD (SO, NO PHONES, COMPUTERS, LIGHTS, TELEVISION, AIR CONDITIONING)?

WHAT WOULD YOU DO?

WHAT WOULD YOUR DAY BE LIKE IF THERE WERE NO ELECTRICITY
IN THE WORLD (SO, NO PHONES, COMPUTERS, LIGHTS,
TELEVISION, AIR CONDITIONING)?

WHAT WOULD YOU DO?

MY FAVORITE KIND OF WEATHER IS:

I DON'T LIKE DAYS THAT ARE TOO:

I'D LOVE TO LIVE IN A CLIMATE LIKE:

MY FAVORITE KIND OF WEATHER IS:

I DON'T LIKE DAYS THAT ARE TOO:

I'D LOVE TO LIVE IN A CLIMATE LIKE:

LIKE & DISLIKE

	✓	X
SPORT		
TV SHOW		
MOVIE		
ACTIVITY		
FRUIT		
VEGETABLE		
SEASON		
CAKE FLAVOR		
CANDLE SCENT		
COLOR		

· ME ·

FOR EACH ENTRY, WRITE A TYPE YOU
LIKE AND A TYPE YOU DISLIKE.

	✓	X
SPORT		
TV SHOW		
MOVIE		
ACTIVITY		
FRUIT		
VEGETABLE		
SEASON		
CAKE FLAVOR		
CANDLE SCENT		
COLOR		

CREATE A PIE CHART ACCORDING TO HOW MUCH TIME PER WEEK YOU SPEND ON EACH ACTIVITY. MAKE A COLOR KEY OR LABEL YOUR PIE CHART.

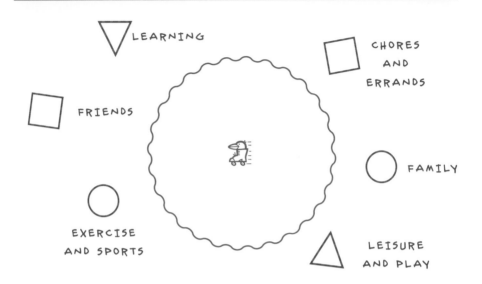

LEARNING

CHORES AND ERRANDS

FRIENDS

FAMILY

EXERCISE AND SPORTS

LEISURE AND PLAY

NOW COLOR IN THE PIE ACCORDING TO HOW MUCH TIME YOU WOULD IDEALLY LIKE TO SPEND ON EACH ACTIVITY.

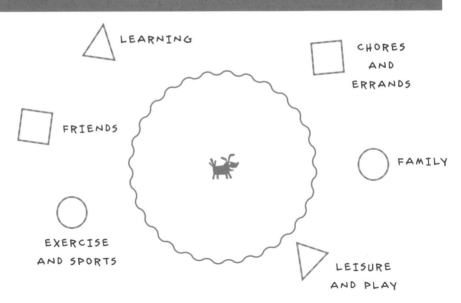

LEARNING

CHORES AND ERRANDS

FRIENDS

FAMILY

EXERCISE AND SPORTS

LEISURE AND PLAY

CREATE A PIE CHART ACCORDING TO HOW MUCH TIME PER WEEK YOU SPEND ON EACH ACTIVITY. MAKE A COLOR KEY OR LABEL YOUR PIE CHART.

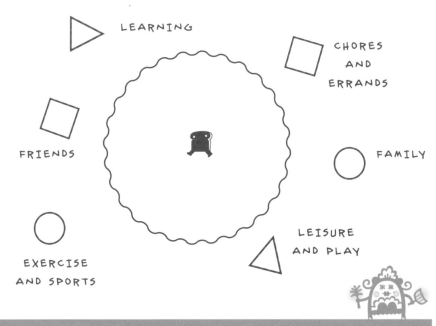

NOW COLOR IN THE PIE ACCORDING TO HOW MUCH TIME YOU WOULD IDEALLY LIKE TO SPEND ON EACH ACTIVITY.

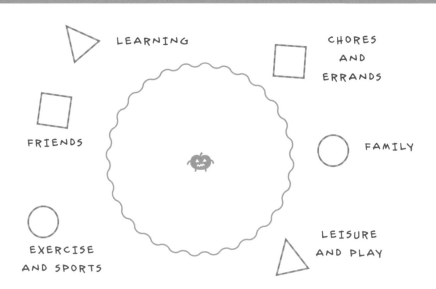

WHAT IS YOUR FAVORITE WAY TO SPEND THE DAY?

DRAW YOURSELF DURING THAT DAY.

WHAT IS YOUR FAVORITE WAY TO SPEND THE DAY?

DRAW YOURSELF DURING THAT DAY.

WHAT MAKES A GOOD FRIEND?

DESCRIBE THE BEST THING ABOUT YOUR BEST FRIEND.

WHAT MAKES A GOOD FRIEND?

DESCRIBE THE BEST THING ABOUT YOUR BEST FRIEND.

MOM

✓OR X WHETHER YOU LIKE OR
DISLIKE SOMETHING IN YOUR
COLUMN FOR EACH ENTRY.

✓LIKE OR X DISLIKE?

CLASSICAL MUSIC	
BABY CARROTS	
AUTUMN LEAVES	
YOGA	
OUTDOOR PICNICS	
POLAROIDS	
SLEEPOVERS	
TENNIS	
SORBET	
VIDEO GAMES	
COMIC BOOKS	

✓OR X WHETHER YOU LIKE OR
DISLIKE SOMETHING IN YOUR
COLUMN FOR EACH ENTRY.

ME

✓LIKE OR X DISLIKE?

CLASSICAL MUSIC		
BABY CARROTS		
AUTUMN LEAVES		
YOGA		
OUTDOOR PICNICS		
POLAROIDS		
SLEEPOVERS		
TENNIS		
SORBET		
VIDEO GAMES		
COMIC BOOKS		

THREE WAYS WE'RE ALIKE:

1

2

3

THREE WAYS WE'RE DIFFERENT:

1

2

3

THREE WAYS WE'RE ALIKE:

1

~~~~~~

2

~~~~~~

3

THREE WAYS WE'RE DIFFERENT:

1

~~~~~~

2

~~~~~~

3

~~~~~~

DESIGN A VIDEO GAME OR A BOARD GAME. WHAT KIND OF GAME WOULD YOU MAKE?

DRAW THE CHARACTERS OR THE GAMEBOARD.

DESIGN A VIDEO GAME OR A BOARD GAME. WHAT KIND OF GAME WOULD YOU MAKE?

DRAW THE CHARACTERS OR THE GAMEBOARD.

DRAW A PORTRAIT OF YOURSELF AT DIFFERENT STAGES OF YOUR LIFE.

PRESENT self.

FUTURE self.

PAST self.

Draw your past self (who you were when you were younger). Your present self (who you are now), and your future self (who you want to be when you're older).

PAST self.

FUTURE self.

PRESENT self.

LIKE & DISLIKE

	✓	X
VIDEOGAME		
BOOK SERIES		
SONG		
TASTE		
SMELL		
SOUND		
TEXTURE		
CITY		
VACATION		
RESTAURANT		

FOR EACH ENTRY, WRITE A TYPE YOU
LIKE AND A TYPE YOU DISLIKE.

	✓	X
VIDEOGAME		
BOOK SERIES		
SONG		
TASTE		
SMELL		
SOUND		
TEXTURE		
CITY		
VACATION		
RESTAURANT		

THREE WAYS TO MAKE LIFE MORE ADVENTUROUS

· MOM ·

1

2

3

BUCKET LIST ADVENTURES

· MOM ·

1

2

3

THREE WAYS TO MAKE LIFE
MORE ADVENTUROUS

· ME ·

1

2

3

BUCKET LIST ADVENTURES

· ME ·

1

2

3

Pick the person who has had the most influence on your life over the last year and draw them below.

· MOM ·

PERSON of the YEAR

Pick the person who has had the most influence on your life over the last year and draw them below.

· ME ·

PERSON of the YEAR

#1

FAMILY PROJECTS
· MOM ·

GARDEN

HOME

CRAFTS

HOLIDAY DECORATING

FAMILY PROJECTS
· ME ·

GARDEN

HOME

CRAFTS

HOLIDAY DECORATING

I'M TRYING TO BE MORE...

☐ KIND

☐ PATIENT

☐ THOUGHTFUL

☐ HONEST

☐ PLAYFUL

☐ STRONG

☐ SMART

☐ _____

☐ _____

☐ _____

WHEN GROW UP, I WANT TO BE...

☐ KIND

☐ PATIENT

☐ A GOOD LISTENER

☐ HONEST

☐ PLAYFUL

☐ STRONG

☐ SMART

☐ _____

☐ _____

☐ _____

MY FAVORITE MEMORY OF MY PARENTS:

MY FAVORITE MEMORY OF OR STORY
ABOUT MY GRANDPARENTS:

THINGS TO TRY

· MOM ·   · ME ·

CLASS I'D
LIKE TO
TAKE:

NEW SKILL
I WANT TO
LEARN:

FOOD I
WANT TO
TRY:

CONCERT
OR SHOW
I'D LIKE TO
SEE:

GAME I WANT
TO PLAY:

Everybody has at least one thing that they are proud of one feature that they most identify with.

· MOM ·

consider the traits that you are proud of
and make you who you are. Draw your
greatest strength.

·ME·

CIRCLE YOUR ANSWERS
THEN POSE YOUR OWN QUESTIONS ON THE
OPPOSITE PAGE FOR YOUR JOURNAL MATE.

WOULD YOU RATHER...

Ride a horse or a motorcycle?

 vacation at the beach or
in the mountains?

Go camping or
stay in a fancy hotel?

Swim in a pool or a lake?

Cross a stream by balancing on a log
or hopping across rocks?

Give up tv and videos for a year or
give up desserts and candy for a year?

Mashed potatoes or french fries?

1

2

3

4

5

6

1

2

3

4

5

6

CIRCLE YOUR ANSWERS
THEN POSE YOUR OWN QUESTIONS ON THE
OPPOSITE PAGE FOR YOUR JOURNAL MATE.

WOULD YOU RATHER...

Ride a horse or a motorcycle?

vacation at the beach or
in the mountains?

Go camping or
stay in a fancy hotel?

swim in a pool or a lake?

cross a stream by balancing on a log
or hopping across rocks?

Give up tv and videos for a year or
give up desserts and candy for a year?

mashed potatoes or french fries?

we all have ideas about the kind of place we would like to live in.

MOM

If I could live in my dream home, this is what it
would look like:

ME

FAVORITE CHARACTERS

BOOK CHARACTERS:

MOVIE CHARACTERS:

CARTOON CHARACTERS:

FAVORITE CHARACTERS

BOOK CHARACTERS:

MOVIE CHARACTERS:

CARTOON CHARACTERS:

NAME A FAMILY MEMBER WHO

	· MOM ·	· ME ·
ISN'T AFRAID OF ANYTHING:		
GIVES THE BEST GIFTS:		
LOVES HOLIDAYS:		
IS THE MOST DRAMATIC:		
TELLS A GOOD STORY:		
LIVES THE FURTHEST:		
LOVES ANIMALS:		

ONE TREASURED ITEM I'D LIKE TO PASS DOWN TO YOU IS:

· MOM ·

ONE TREASURED ITEM I'D LIKE TO INHERIT FROM YOU IS:

· ME ·

1 ----TO----- 10

1 2 3 4 5 6 7 8 9 10	BRUSSEL SPROUTS
1 2 3 4 5 6 7 8 9 10	BOARD GAMES
1 2 3 4 5 6 7 8 9 10	MUSICALS
1 2 3 4 5 6 7 8 9 10	AUTUMN
1 2 3 4 5 6 7 8 9 10	HISTORY
1 2 3 4 5 6 7 8 9 10	STICKERS
1 2 3 4 5 6 7 8 9 10	SOCCER
1 2 3 4 5 6 7 8 9 10	RUNNING
1 2 3 4 5 6 7 8 9 10	SNAKES
1 2 3 4 5 6 7 8 9 10	CORNDOGS
1 2 3 4 5 6 7 8 9 10	TROPHIES
1 2 3 4 5 6 7 8 9 10	SPRINKLES
1 2 3 4 5 6 7 8 9 10	ANIMATED MOVIES
1 2 3 4 5 6 7 8 9 10	ARTS AND CRAFTS
1 2 3 4 5 6 7 8 9 10	ROAD TRIPS
1 2 3 4 5 6 7 8 9 10	CLOWNS

RATE THE FOLLOWING THINGS,
FROM ONE TO TEN,
AND COMPARE YOUR ANSWERS.

1	2	3	4	5	6	7	8	9	10	BRUSSEL SPROUTS
1	2	3	4	5	6	7	8	9	10	BOARD GAMES
1	2	3	4	5	6	7	8	9	10	MUSICALS
1	2	3	4	5	6	7	8	9	10	AUTUMN
1	2	3	4	5	6	7	8	9	10	HISTORY
1	2	3	4	5	6	7	8	9	10	STICKERS
1	2	3	4	5	6	7	8	9	10	SOCCER
1	2	3	4	5	6	7	8	9	10	RUNNING
1	2	3	4	5	6	7	8	9	10	SNAKES
1	2	3	4	5	6	7	8	9	10	CORNDOGS
1	2	3	4	5	6	7	8	9	10	TROPHIES
1	2	3	4	5	6	7	8	9	10	SPRINKLES
1	2	3	4	5	6	7	8	9	10	ANIMATED MOVIES
1	2	3	4	5	6	7	8	9	10	ARTS AND CRAFTS
1	2	3	4	5	6	7	8	9	10	ROAD TRIPS
1	2	3	4	5	6	7	8	9	10	CLOWNS

IF YOU COULD MAKE YOURSELF INTO A SUPERHERO, WHAT NAME WOULD YOU GIVE YOURSELF?

WHAT WOULD YOUR SUPERPOWERS BE?

IF YOU COULD MAKE YOURSELF INTO A SUPERHERO, WHAT
NAME WOULD YOU GIVE YOURSELF?

WHAT WOULD YOUR SUPERPOWERS BE?

There are times in our lives when we make mistakes and need forgiveness.

· MOM ·

Forgiveness is something we give and receive, both to others and to ourselves. Draw something that you feel you need forgiveness for.

· ME ·

A GENIE APPEARS AND GRANTS YOU THREE WISHES. WHAT WOULD YOU WISH FOR? (YOU CAN'T USE ANY FOR MORE WISHES!)

1

2

3

A GENIE APPEARS AND GRANTS YOU THREE WISHES. WHAT WOULD YOU WISH FOR? (YOU CAN'T USE ANY FOR MORE WISHES!)

1

2

3

MY FAVORITE CHILDHOOD...

TOY:

PICTURE BOOK:

CHAPTER BOOK:

POEM:

TEACHER:

SCHOOL SUBJECT:

PET:

COLOR:

OUTFIT:

MEAL:

CARTOON:

GAME:

MY FAVORITE CHILDHOOD...

TOY:

PICTURE BOOK:

CHAPTER BOOK:

POEM:

TEACHER:

SCHOOL
SUBJECT:

PET:

COLOR:

OUTFIT:

MEAL:

CARTOON:

GAME:

Imagine finding a hidden magic shop and the magician who owns it offers to gift you anything in his shop.

What would you choose? your choice can
be something tangible (something that can be
touched) or intangible (something that cannot
be touched). Draw what you would choose on
the shelf below.

WHAT IS THE MOST DIFFICULT PART OF BEING THE AGE YOU ARE NOW?

DO YOU THINK THAT ASPECT WILL GET EASIER OR HARDER AS YOU GET OLDER?

WHAT IS THE MOST DIFFICULT PART OF BEING THE AGE YOU ARE NOW?

DO YOU THINK THAT ASPECT WILL GET EASIER OR HARDER AS YOU GET OLDER?

consider what values are important to you.

· MOM ·

Draw a picture of yourself using one
of these values in your everyday life.

· ME ·

CIRCLE YOUR ANSWERS
THEN POSE YOUR OWN QUESTIONS ON THE
OPPOSITE PAGE FOR YOUR JOURNAL MATE.

WOULD YOU RATHER...

Live in a cozy cottage or
a grand manor house?

Be an only child or
have nine siblings?

work on a solo project or
work on a group project?

Be way too busy or completely bored?

Breath underwater or fly?

Invisibility cloak or magic broom?

Aliens or robots?

1

2

3

4

5

6

1

2

3

4

5

6

CIRCLE YOUR ANSWERS

THEN POSE YOUR OWN QUESTIONS ON THE
OPPOSITE PAGE FOR YOUR JOURNAL MATE.

WOULD YOU RATHER...

Live in a cozy cottage or
a grand manor house?

Be an only child or
have nine siblings?

work on a solo project or
work on a group project?

Be way too busy or completely bored?

Breath underwater or fly?

Invisibility cloak or magic broom?

Aliens or robots?

OF ALL OUR FAMILY TRADITIONS,
WHICH ONE IS YOUR FAVORITE?

WHAT MAKES IT SO SPECIAL TO YOU?

OF ALL OUR FAMILY TRADITIONS,
WHICH ONE IS YOUR FAVORITE?

WHAT MAKES IT SO SPECIAL TO YOU?

Think about animals and what traits that you may have observed in them.

• MOM •

Then draw a portrait of your family, but as the animals you associate with them based on their particular traits. consider their external traits, like appearance and behavior, and internal traits, like personality.

· ° ME ° ·

WHAT HOLIDAY DO YOU MOST CHERISH?

DESCRIBE THE SIGHTS

DESCRIBE THE SOUNDS

DESCRIBE THE SMELLS

DESCRIBE THE RITUALS

WHAT DO YOU DO TOGETHER AS A FAMILY TO CELEBRATE?

DESCRIBE THE SIGHTS

DESCRIBE THE SOUNDS

DESCRIBE THE SMELLS

DESCRIBE THE RITUALS

Bridges connect places that were previously separate, allowing us to easily travel. Think about what kind of bridge you would build and the places that it would connect.

Draw your bridge and the things that it connects together.

WHAT IS YOUR FAVORITE TIME OF YEAR?

DRAW THE BEST PARTS.

WHAT IS YOUR FAVORITE TIME OF YEAR?

DRAW THE BEST PARTS.

✔ LIKE OR X DISLIKE?

✓ OR X WHETHER YOU LIKE OR DISLIKE
SOMETHING IN YOUR COLUMN FOR EACH ENTRY.

	· MOM ·	· ME ·
SPRING		
DESSERTS		
PETS		
SHORT HAIR		
BOWLING ALLEYS		
LATE NIGHTS		
MALLS		
RANCH		
OLD MOVIES		
SCIENCE-FICTION		

NAME THE FAMILY MEMBER WHO...

· MOM ·   · ME ·

	MOM	ME
GIVES THE BEST ADVICE		
HAS THE LONGEST HAIR		
ALWAYS SPEAKS THEIR MIND		
LIKES TO BE OUTDOORS		
IS ALWAYS POSITIVE		
LOVES ADVENTURE		

1 ---TO--- 👉 10

1	2	3	4	5	6	7	8	9	10		CATS
1	2	3	4	5	6	7	8	9	10		COLORFUL HAIR
1	2	3	4	5	6	7	8	9	10		HOT CHOCOLATE
1	2	3	4	5	6	7	8	9	10		FUZZY SWEATERS
1	2	3	4	5	6	7	8	9	10		THE MOON
1	2	3	4	5	6	7	8	9	10		LLAMAS
1	2	3	4	5	6	7	8	9	10		VINTAGE CLOTHES
1	2	3	4	5	6	7	8	9	10		KNITTING
1	2	3	4	5	6	7	8	9	10		CAMPFIRES
1	2	3	4	5	6	7	8	9	10		HEIGHTS
1	2	3	4	5	6	7	8	9	10		SHARKS
1	2	3	4	5	6	7	8	9	10		PIRATES
1	2	3	4	5	6	7	8	9	10		RACCOONS
1	2	3	4	5	6	7	8	9	10		OATMEAL
1	2	3	4	5	6	7	8	9	10		HONEY
1	2	3	4	5	6	7	8	9	10		NINJAS

RATE THE FOLLOWING THINGS, FROM ONE TO TEN, AND COMPARE YOUR ANSWERS.

1	2	3	4	5	6	7	8	9	10	CATS
1	2	3	4	5	6	7	8	9	10	COLORFUL HAIR
1	2	3	4	5	6	7	8	9	10	HOT CHOCOLATE
1	2	3	4	5	6	7	8	9	10	FUZZY SWEATERS
1	2	3	4	5	6	7	8	9	10	THE MOON
1	2	3	4	5	6	7	8	9	10	LLAMAS
1	2	3	4	5	6	7	8	9	10	VINTAGE CLOTHES
1	2	3	4	5	6	7	8	9	10	KNITTING
1	2	3	4	5	6	7	8	9	10	CAMPFIRES
1	2	3	4	5	6	7	8	9	10	HEIGHTS
1	2	3	4	5	6	7	8	9	10	SHARKS
1	2	3	4	5	6	7	8	9	10	PIRATES
1	2	3	4	5	6	7	8	9	10	RACCOONS
1	2	3	4	5	6	7	8	9	10	OATMEAL
1	2	3	4	5	6	7	8	9	10	HONEY
1	2	3	4	5	6	7	8	9	10	NINJAS

WHAT ARE YOUR FAVORITE TREATS?

DRAW YOUR FAVORITE TREATS AND SPECIAL THINGS.

WHAT ARE YOUR FAVORITE TREATS?

DRAW YOUR FAVORITE TREATS AND SPECIAL THINGS.

Amusement parks are fun to visit and there are so many types of rides to enjoy.

Think about what kind of ride best represents your life right now and draw it below.

· ME ·

SOME THINGS THAT REALLY ANNOY ME:

SOME THINGS THAT MAKE ME LAUGH:

ONE THING I'M AFRAID OF:

SOME THINGS THAT REALLY ANNOY ME:

SOME THINGS THAT MAKE ME LAUGH:

ONE THING I'M AFRAID OF:

CIRCLE YOUR ANSWERS

THEN POSE YOUR OWN QUESTIONS ON THE
OPPOSITE PAGE FOR YOUR JOURNAL MATE.

WOULD YOU RATHER...

Run or walk?

Laser vision or
x-ray vision?

summer or winter?

Ninjas or pirates?

 North or south?

Plaid or solid colors?

chicken nuggets or
fish sticks?

ketchup or mustard?

1

2

3

4

5

6

1

2

3

4

5

6

CIRCLE YOUR ANSWERS

THEN POSE YOUR OWN QUESTIONS ON THE
OPPOSITE PAGE FOR YOUR JOURNAL MATE.

WOULD YOU RATHER...

Run or walk?

Laser vision or
x-ray vision?

Summer or winter?

Ninjas or pirates?

North or South?

Plaid or solid colors?

chicken nuggets or
fish sticks?

ketchup or mustard?

· MOM ·

If you could create your own invention, what would it be?

Draw it in the space below.

MOM ♥

FOR EACH ENTRY, WRITE
A TYPE YOU LIKE AND A
TYPE YOU DISLIKE.

LIKE AND DISLIKE

	LIKE	DISLIKE
HAIR COLOR		
OUTFIT/ CLOTHING		
ALBUM		
HOLIDAY		
CHIP FLAVOR		
CLASS		
PLANET		
WILD ANIMAL		
FLOWER		
PET		
SEASON		

ME

FOR EACH ENTRY, WRITE
A TYPE YOU LIKE AND A
TYPE YOU DISLIKE.

LIKE AND DISLIKE

HAIR COLOR		
OUTFIT/ CLOTHING		
ALBUM		
HOLIDAY		
CHIP FLAVOR		
CLASS		
PLANET		
WILD ANIMAL		
FLOWER		
PET		
SEASON		

179

IF YOU COULD VISIT ANY PLACE IN THE WORLD,
WHERE WOULD YOU GO?

make x marks on the map and
draw the place you want to visit.

DO YOU LIKE TO BE SCARED BY CREEPY
CAMPFIRE STORIES?

DRAW SOMETHING SPOOKY IF YOU DO AND SOMETHING
CHEERY IF YOU DON'T.

DO YOU LIKE TO BE SCARED BY CREEPY
CAMPFIRE STORIES?

DRAW SOMETHING SPOOKY IF YOU DO AND SOMETHING
CHEERY IF YOU DON'T.

· MOM ·

Invite the people you trust to your how over for dinner.

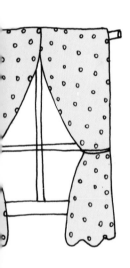

Draw them around the table and think about why it is that you trust them.

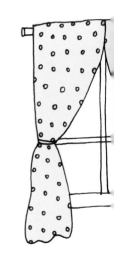

CIRCLE YOUR ANSWERS
THEN POSE YOUR OWN QUESTIONS ON THE
OPPOSITE PAGE FOR YOUR JOURNAL MATE.

WOULD YOU RATHER...

own a pet shark or
a pet bear?

Bungee jumping or
parachuting?

Rollerblading or ice-skating?

Guitar or drums?

Boots or sneakers?

Hats or no hats?

Fall or spring?

Pens or pencils?

1

2

3

4

5

6

1

2

3

4

5

6

CIRCLE YOUR ANSWERS

THEN POSE YOUR OWN QUESTIONS ON THE
OPPOSITE PAGE FOR YOUR JOURNAL MATE.

WOULD YOU RATHER...

own a pet shark or
a pet bear?

Bungee jumping or
parachuting?

Rollerblading or ice-skating?

Guitar or drums?

Boots or sneakers?

Hats or no hats?

Fall or spring?

pens or pencils?

✔ LIKE AND ✘ DISLIKE?

☐ INSECTS

☐ GYM/EXERCISE CLASS

☐ RAINY DAYS

☐ SELFIES

☐ BOY BANDS

☐ ROLLER COASTERS

☐ BEACH

☐ BROCCOLI

☐ CHEESE

☐ SUPERHERO MOVIES

✔OR X WHETHER YOU LIKE OR DISLIKE
SOMETHING IN YOUR COLUMN FOR EACH ENTRY.

☐ INSECTS

☐ GYM/EXERCISE CLASS

☐ RAINY DAYS

☐ SELFIES

☐ BOY BANDS

☐ ROLLER COASTERS

☐ BEACH

☐ BROCCOLI

☐ CHEESE

☐ SUPERHERO MOVIES

A HABIT I WANT TO FORM:

A HABIT I WANT TO BREAK:

A HABIT I WANT TO FORM:

A HABIT I WANT TO BREAK:

✔ LIKE OR X DISLIKE?

✔ OR X WHETHER YOU LIKE OR DISLIKE
SOMETHING IN YOUR COLUMN FOR EACH ENTRY.

♥ ♥ ♥ ♥ ♥

	· MOM ·	· ME ·
MOVIE THEATRES		
PERIOD DRAMAS		
TWINKLE LIGHTS		
WINTER OLYMPICS		
LONG CAR RIDES		
AUTUMN		
CAFES		
LIVE CONCERTS		
BUBBLE GUM		
FAST FOOD		

194

NAME A FAMILY MEMBER WHO

	· MOM ·	· ME ·
ALWAYS LISTENS TO MUSIC		
READS THE MOST BOOKS		
WOULD BE A GOOD POLITICIAN		
PLAYS AN INSTRUMENT		
KNOWS THE BEST PLACES TO EAT		
WOULD MOST LIKELY KNOW SOMEONE FAMOUS		
TRAVELS THE MOST		

WHAT IS THE MOST FUN YOU'VE EVER HAD? DESCRIBE THE DAY.

WHO WERE YOU WITH?

WHAT IS THE MOST FUN YOU'VE EVER HAD? DESCRIBE THE DAY.

WHO WERE YOU WITH?

INVENT AN AWESOME DESSERT. WHAT INGREDIENTS GO INTO IT AND HOW IS IT PREPARED?

WHAT WILL YOU CALL YOUR CREATION?

INVENT AN AWESOME DESSERT. WHAT INGREDIENTS GO
INTO IT AND HOW IS IT PREPARED?

WHAT WILL YOU CALL YOUR CREATION?

USE THE SPACE BELOW TO CREATE
A SYMMETRICAL MANDALA DESIGN.

IF YOU'RE NOT SURE WHAT TO DRAW, TRY REPEATING A SHAPE,
IMAGE, OR PATTERN WITHIN THE CIRCLE AND SEE IF YOU FEEL
RELAXED WHILE YOUR CREATE IT.

DATE COMPLETED:

my favorite parts of journaling with my child:

My favorite parts of journaling with my mom:

Inspiring | Educating | Creating | Entertaining

Brimming with creative inspiration, how-to projects, and useful information to enrich your everyday life, Quarto Knows is a favorite destination for those pursuing their interests and passions. Visit our site and dig deeper with our books into your area of interest: Quarto Creates, Quarto Cooks, Quarto Homes, Quarto Lives, Quarto Drives, Quarto Explores, Quarto Gifts, or Quarto Kids.

THIS EDITION PUBLISHED IN 2021 BY CHARTWELL BOOKS,
AN IMPRINT OF THE QUARTO GROUP,
142 WEST 36TH STREET, 4TH FLOOR,
NEW YORK, NY 10018, USA
T (212) 779-4972 F (212) 779-6058
WWW.QUARTOKNOWS.COM

PREVIOUSLY PUBLISHED IN 2021 BY CHARTWELL BOOKS, AN IMPRINT OF THE QUARTO GROUP,
142 WEST 36TH STREET, 4TH FLOOR, NEW YORK, NY 10018, USA

CHARTWELL TITLES ARE ALSO AVAILABLE AT DISCOUNT FOR RETAIL, WHOLESALE, PROMOTIONAL, AND BULK PURCHASE. FOR DETAILS, CONTACT THE SPECIAL SALES MANAGER BY EMAIL AT SPECIALSALES@QUARTO.COM OR BY MAIL AT THE QUARTO GROUP, ATTN: SPECIAL SALES MANAGER, 100 CUMMINGS CENTER, SUITE 265D, BEVERLY, MA 01915, USA.

10 9 8 7 6 5 4 3 2 1

ISBN: 978-0-7858-4038-1

PUBLISHER: RAGE KINDELSPERGER
CREATIVE DIRECTOR: LAURA DREW
MANAGING EDITOR: CARA DONALDSON
PROJECT EDITOR: LEEANN MOREAU
EDITORIAL INTERNS: ALMA GOMEZ MARTINEZ & YASHU PERICHERLA
TEXT: SUSAN LAUZAU
COVER DESIGN: BETH MIDDLEWORTH
INTERIOR DESIGN: BETH MIDDLEWORTH

PRINTED IN CHINA